1
american popular piano
SKILLS

Created by
Dr. Scott
McBride Smith

Series Composer
Christopher
Norton

Editor
Dr. Scott
McBride Smith

Associate Editor
Clarke
MacIntosh

Book Design & Engraving
Andrew Jones

Cover Design
Wagner Design

Introduction

Everyone agrees that Tiger Woods is one of the greatest golfers of all time. Some even think he is the best ever! He won the 1997 Masters Tournament when he was 21 years old, the youngest winner in history. He was also the youngest golfer to complete a career *Grand Slam*, winning all four major championships by the age of 25.

How did he do it? Let's see what he says.

From early childhood I dreamed of being the world's best golfer. I worked hard and applied my family's values to everything I did. Integrity, honesty, discipline, responsiblity and fun; I learned these values at home and in school, each one pushing me further toward my dream.

Eldrick (Tiger) Woods
Letter from Tiger, Tiger Woods Foundation Website
http://www.twfound.org

The best way to achieve [a] goal is through sound fundamentals.

Tiger Woods
Golf Digest, November 1998

What's your dream? Do you want to be one of the world's best musicians? play piano for your own enjoyment? or entertain your friends and family? No matter which, Tiger is right. Hard work, responsibility – and fun! – will be the keystones to your success.

In golf, the term "fundamentals" covers many things. In piano playing, we can break it down into three broad groupings.

- **Technic.** This is the ability to readily make the motions that create beautiful sounds. Dynamic control, tonal evenness and variety, and speed would fall into this category.

- **Sightreading.** You might also call these "quick learning" skills. Seeing patterns, noticing details, and playing without stopping – right away.

- **Listening.** This is perhaps the most important of all! If you can't hear the sounds of a piece in your mind before you play, you will never do a good job performing it. Psychologists call this "audiation".

Do you think practicing basic skills is boring? Get over it!

Your playing will never be as good or as enjoyable as you want it to be if your basic skills are not excellent. Every athlete – including Tiger – spends time on drills, exercises and warm-ups outside of the game. Pianists should, too. When your piano fundamentals become strong, you will learn everything more easily and perform more confidently.

This book is designed to help, but it won't work if you don't! Practice carefully and frequently. Spend some time every day on your basic skills and, who knows ... you may become the Tiger Woods of the piano.

Library and Archives Canada Cataloguing in Publication

Smith, Scott McBride

American popular piano [music] : skills / created by Scott McBride Smith ;
series composer, Christopher Norton ;
editor, Scott McBride Smith ; associate editor, Clarke MacIntosh.

To be complete in 11 volumes.
Contents: Preparatory level -- Level 1 -- Level 2.
Miscellaneous information: The series is organized in 11 levels, from preparatory to level 10, each including a repertoire album,
an etudes album, a skills book, and an instrumental backings compact disc.

ISBN 978-1-897379-22-6 (preparatory level).--ISBN 978-1-897379-23-3 (level 1).--
ISBN 978-1-897379-24-0 (level 2)

1. Piano--Studies and exercises. 2. Piano--Studies and exercises--Juvenile.
I. Norton, Christopher, 1953- II. MacIntosh, S. Clarke, 1959- III. Title.

LEVEL ① SKILLS

Table of Contents

Unit One - Module One

A. Brainthumpers

Practice daily.

1) Play while counting out loud.

2)

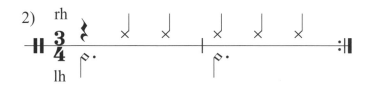

Tap this rhythmic pattern while counting out loud.
How many notes are in the left hand?_____

B. Technic

Practice Daily.
For directions, see *How to Use This Book* on page 46.

1) Pentascales (pages 42-43)

   No. ____; M.M. ____; S / T ____

   key(s): C F G

   Articulation: *legato staccato portato*

   Dynamic: ***f* *mf* *mp***

2) Triads (pages 44-45)

   No. ____; M.M. ____; S / T ____

   key(s): C F G

   Articulation: *legato staccato portato*

   Dynamic: ***f* *mf* *mp***

C. Prepared Sightreading Piece

Play three times, keeping a steady beat.

For directions, see *How to Use This Book* on page 46.

____ on C?

____ on G?

D. Aural Skills - Rhythmic

Practice daily.

1) ♩ = 60

rh

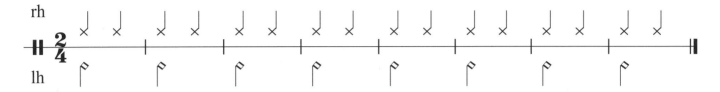

lh

    a)   Tap the left hand then the right hand with the metronome.

    b)   Tap hands together with the metronome.

    c)   Tap hands together and count out loud with the metronome.

2) ♩ = 60

    a)   Clap while counting out loud.

repeat 5x

E. Aural Skills - Pitch

1) Play this triad.

Continue to hold the notes,
while singing pitches: 1-3-5; 5-3-1.

2) Play and hold middle C at the piano.

    a) Sing middle C and match pitch with the piano.

    b) Sing and play the C major pentascale simultaneously. Then sing again without the piano.

    c) Sing the exercise.

3) Play the triad. Sing scale degrees 1-5-1.

Play the phrase at the piano and then sing it back without the piano. Pitch and rhythm should be accurate.

Unit One - Module Two

A. Brainthumpers

Practice daily.

1) Observe the right hand slur.

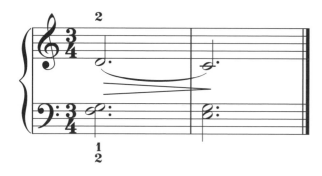

2)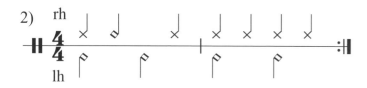

Tap this rhythmic pattern while counting out loud.
How many notes are in the left hand?_____

B. Technic

Practice Daily.
For directions, see *How to Use This Book* on page 46.

1) Pentascales (pages 42-43)

No. ____; M.M. ____; S / T ____

key(s): C F G

Articulation: *legato staccato portato*

Dynamic: **𝆑 𝆐𝆑 𝆐𝆎**

2) Triads (pages 44-45)

No. ____; M.M. ____; S / T ____

key(s): C F G

Articulation: *legato staccato portato*

Dynamic: **𝆑 𝆐𝆑 𝆐𝆎**

C. Prepared Sightreading Piece

Play three times, keeping a steady beat.

For directions, see *How to Use This Book* on page 46.

D. Aural Skills - Rhythmic

Practice daily.

1) ♩ = 92

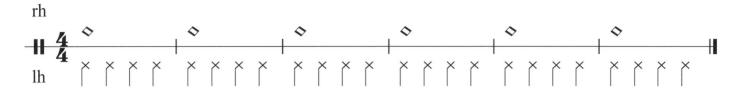

rh

lh

a) Tap the left hand then the right hand with the metronome.
b) Tap hands together with the metronome.
c) Tap hands together and count out loud with the metronome.

2) ♩ = 92

a) Clap while counting out loud.

repeat 5x

E. Aural Skills - Pitch

1) Play this triad.

Continue to hold the notes,
while singing pitches: 1-5-3; 5-3-1.

2) Play and hold middle C at the piano.

a) Sing middle C and match pitch with the piano.
b) Sing and play the C major pentascale simultaneously. Then sing again without the piano.
c) Sing the exercise.

3) Play the triad. Sing scale degrees 1-5-1.

Play the phrase at the piano and then sing it back without the piano. Pitch and rhythm should be accurate.

Unit One - Module Three

A. Brainthumpers

Practice daily.

1) Play while counting out loud.

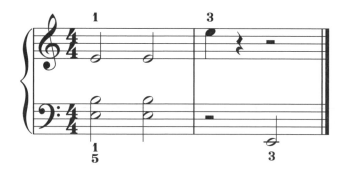

2) rh

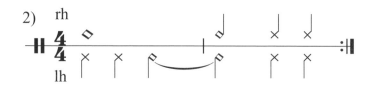

lh

Tap this rhythmic pattern while counting out loud.
How many notes are in the left hand?_____

C. Prepared Sightreading Piece

Play three times, keeping a steady beat.

For directions, see *How to
Use This Book* on page 46.

____ on F?

____ on F?

D. Aural Skills - Rhythmic

Practice daily.

1) ♩ = 48

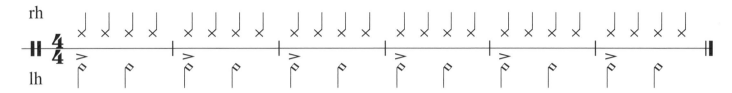

a) Tap the left hand then the right hand with the metronome.

b) Tap hands together with the metronome.

c) Tap hands together and count out loud with the metronome.

2) ♩ = 48

a) Clap while counting out loud.

repeat 5x

E. Aural Skills - Pitch

1) Play this triad.

Continue to hold the notes,
while singing pitches: 5-3-1; 1-3-5.

2) Play and hold middle C at the piano.

a) Sing middle C and match pitch with the piano.

b) Sing and play the C major pentascale simultaneously. Then sing again without the piano.

c) Sing the exercise.

3) Play the triad. Sing scale degrees 1-5-1.

Play the phrase at the piano and then sing it back without the piano. Pitch and rhythm should be accurate.

Unit One - Module Four

A. Brainthumpers

Practice daily.

1) Observe the articulation marks.

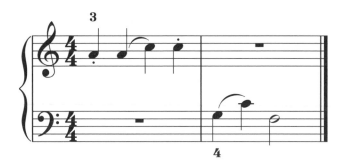

2)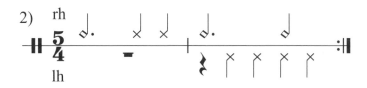

Tap this rhythmic pattern while counting out loud.
How many notes are in the left hand?_____

B. Technic

Practice Daily.
For directions, see *How to Use This Book* on page 46.

1) Pentascales (pages 42-43)

No. ____ ; M.M. ____ ; S / T ____

key(s): C F G

Articulation: *legato staccato portato*

Dynamic: *f mf mp ff pp*

2) Triads (pages 44-45)

No. ____ ; M.M. ____ ; S / T ____

key(s): C F G

Articulation: *legato staccato portato*

Dynamic: *f mf mp ff pp*

C. Prepared Sightreading Piece

Play three times, keeping a steady beat.

For directions, see *How to Use This Book* on page 46.

____ on F?

____ on F?

D. Aural Skills - Rhythmic

Practice daily.

1) ♩ = 120

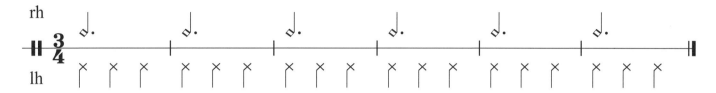

a) Tap the left hand then the right hand with the metronome.

b) Tap hands together with the metronome.

c) Tap hands together and count out loud with the metronome.

2) ♩ = 120

a) Clap while counting out loud.

E. Aural Skills - Pitch

1) Play this triad.

Continue to hold the notes,
while singing pitches: 1-3-5; 3-5-1.

2) Play and hold middle C at the piano.

a) Sing middle C and match pitch with the piano.

b) Sing and play the C major pentascale simultaneously. Then sing again without the piano.

c) Sing the exercise.

3) Play the triad. Sing scale degrees 1-5-1.

Play the phrase at the piano and then sing it back without the piano. Pitch and rhythm should be accurate.

Unit Two - Module One

A. Brainthumpers

Practice daily.

1) Be careful to hold notes for full value.

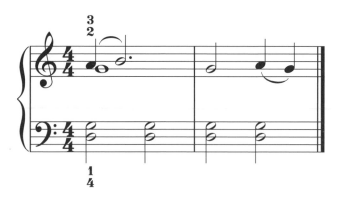

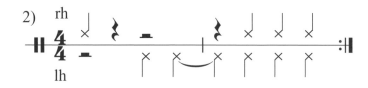

2)

Tap this rhythmic pattern while counting out loud.
How many notes are in the left hand?_____

B. Technic

Practice Daily.

For directions, see *How to Use This Book* on page 46.

1) Pentascales

No. ____ ; M.M. ____ ; S / T ____

key(s): D E A

Articulation: *legato staccato portato*

Dynamic: ***f mf mp***

2) Triads

No. ____ ; M.M. ____ ; S / T ____

key(s): D E A

Articulation: *legato staccato portato*

Dynamic: ***f mf mp***

C. Prepared Sightreading Piece

Play three times, keeping a steady beat.

For directions, see *How to Use This Book* on page 46.

____ on F?

____ on E?

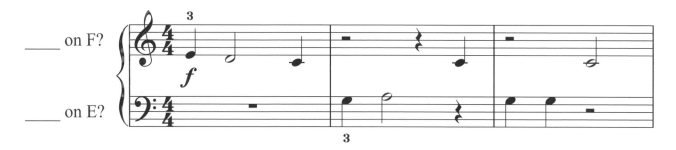

D. Aural Skills - Rhythmic

Practice daily.

1) ♩ = 138

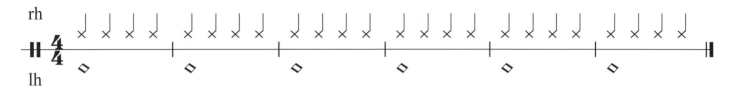

    a) Tap the left hand then the right hand with the metronome.

    b) Tap hands together with the metronome.

    c) Tap hands together and count out loud with the metronome.

2) ♩ = 138

    a) Clap while counting out loud.

E. Aural Skills - Pitch

1) Play this triad.

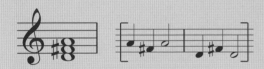

Continue to hold the notes,
while singing pitches: 5-3-5; 1-3-1.

2) Play and hold middle D at the piano.

    a) Sing middle D and match pitch with the piano.

    b) Sing and play the D major pentascale simultaneously. Then sing again without the piano.

    c) Sing the exercise.

3) Play the triad. Sing scale degrees 1-5-1.

Play the phrase at the piano and then sing it back without the piano. Pitch and rhythm should be accurate.

Unit Two - Module Two

A. Brainthumpers

Practice daily.

1) Observe the slurs.

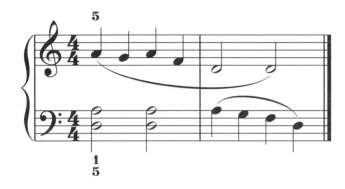

2)

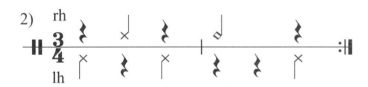

Tap this rhythmic pattern while counting out loud.
How many notes are in the left hand?_____

B. Technic

Practice Daily.

For directions, see *How to Use This Book* on page 46.

1) Pentascales

No. ____; M.M. ____; S / T ____

key(s): D E A

Articulation: *legato staccato portato*

Dynamic: *f mf mp*

2) Triads

No. ____; M.M. ____; S / T ____

key(s): D E A

Articulation: *legato staccato portato*

Dynamic: *f mf mp*

C. Prepared Sightreading Piece

Play three times, keeping a steady beat.

For directions, see *How to Use This Book* on page 46.

_____ on G?

_____ on F?

D. Aural Skills - Rhythmic

Practice daily.

1) ♩ = 112

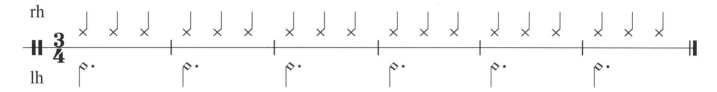

rh

lh

    a)   Tap the left hand then the right hand with the metronome.

    b)   Tap hands together with the metronome.

    c)   Tap hands together and count out loud with the metronome.

2) ♩ = 112

    a)   Clap while counting out loud.

5x

E. Aural Skills - Pitch

1) Play this triad.

Continue to hold the notes,
while singing pitches: 5-3-1; 3-5-1.

2) Play and hold middle D at the piano.

    a) Sing middle D and match pitch with the piano.

    b) Sing and play the D major pentascale simultaneously. Then sing again without the piano.

    c) Sing the exercise.

3) Play the triad. Sing scale degrees 1-5-1.

Play the phrase at the piano and then sing it back without the piano. Pitch and rhythm should be accurate.

Unit Two - Module Three

A. Brainthumpers

Practice daily.

1) Observe the right hand slur.

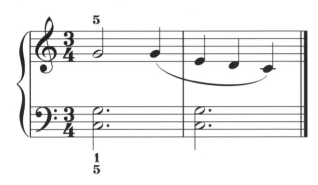

2)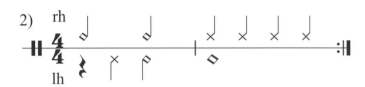

Tap this rhythmic pattern while counting out loud.
How many notes are in the left hand?_____

B. Technic

Practice Daily.
For directions, see *How to Use This Book* on page 46.

1) Pentascales

No. ____; M.M. ____; S / T ____

key(s): D E A

Articulation: *legato staccato portato*

Dynamic: *f mf mp ff*

2) Triads

No. ____; M.M. ____; S / T ____

key(s): D E A

Articulation: *legato staccato portato*

Dynamic: *f mf mp ff*

C. Prepared Sightreading Piece

Play three times, keeping a steady beat.

For directions, see *How to Use This Book* on page 46.

____ on F?

____ on E?

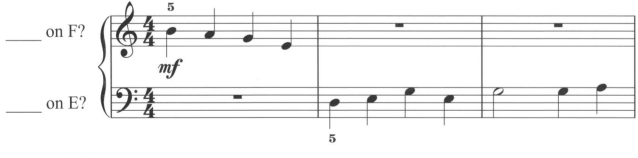

D. Aural Skills - Rhythmic

Practice daily.

1) ♩ = 100

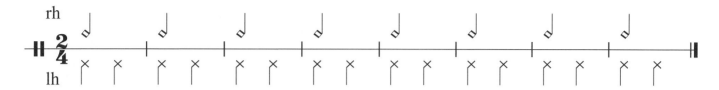

a) Tap the left hand then the right hand with the metronome.

b) Tap hands together with the metronome.

c) Tap hands together and count out loud with the metronome.

2) ♩ = 100

a) Clap while counting out loud.

E. Aural Skills - Pitch

1) Play this triad.

Continue to hold the notes,
while singing pitches: 1-5-5; 5-3-1.

2) Play and hold middle D at the piano.

    a) Sing middle D and match pitch with the piano.

    b) Sing and play the D major pentascale
    simultaneously. Then sing again
    without the piano.

    c) Sing the exercise.

3) Play the triad. Sing scale degrees 1-5-1.

Play the phrase at the piano and then sing it back without the piano. Pitch and rhythm should be accurate.

Unit Two - Module Four

A. Brainthumpers

Practice daily.

1) Observe the slurs.

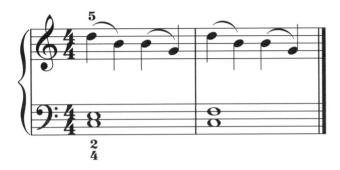

B. Technic

Practice Daily.

For directions, see *How to Use This Book* on page 46.

1) Pentascales

No. _____; M.M. _____; S / T _____

key(s): D E A

Articulation: *legato staccato portato*

Dynamic: *f mf mp ff pp*

2) Triads

No. _____; M.M. _____; S / T _____

key(s): D E A

Articulation: *legato staccato portato*

Dynamic: *f mf mp ff pp*

2)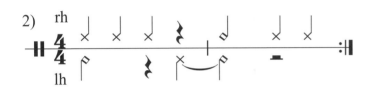

Tap this rhythmic pattern while counting out loud.
How many notes are in the left hand? _____

C. Prepared Sightreading Piece

Play three times, keeping a steady beat.

For directions, see *How to Use This Book* on page 46.

_____ on D?

_____ on B?

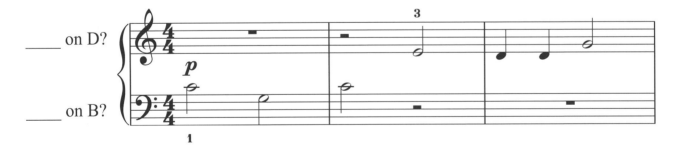

D. Aural Skills - Rhythmic

Practice daily.

1) ♩ = 84

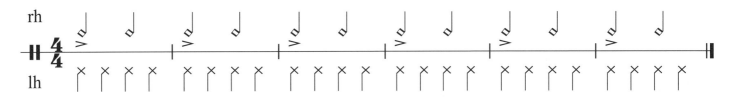

   a) Tap the left hand then the right hand with the metronome.
   b) Tap hands together with the metronome.
   c) Tap hands together and count out loud with the metronome.

2) ♩ = 84

   a) Clap while counting out loud.

E. Aural Skills - Pitch

1) Play this triad.

   Continue to hold the notes,
   while singing pitches: 3-5-1; 3-5-1.

2) Play and hold middle D at the piano.

   a) Sing middle D and match pitch with the piano.

   b) Sing and play the D major pentascale simultaneously. Then sing again without the piano.

   c) Sing the exercise.

3) Play the triad. Sing scale degrees 1-5-1.

   Play the phrase at the piano and then sing it back without the piano. Pitch and rhythm should be accurate.

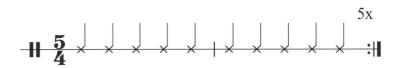

How to Use This Book

The *American Popular Piano Skills* books are designed to be used as a flexible tool for learning the fundamental skills of playing the piano. Research tells us that the most effective way to learn is in small increments, repeated frequently. That's a good thing, considering that many piano students today have very busy schedules and may not have big chunks of time to devote to practice at one time.

How much time should you spend on basic skills? The best choice, of course, is to spend a moderate amount of time daily on technic, sightreading and ear training. But even a smaller amount of time each day, every day is better than spending a lot of time on one day after several days of non-practice.

The Open Plan System

The Open Plan organization of the *American Popular Piano Skills* books encourages skill acquisition at each student's natural pace. Review the chart below to help understand how it works.

How should you schedule assignments of Skills? Progress will vary depending on each student's needs and practice timetable.

- **Faster moving students** can do one module per week.
- **Many students** will work on two or three skill areas within a module each week.
- **Students with less practice time** often do just one skill area.

Areas that need extra work may of course be repeated as necessary.

American Popular Piano
Skills Book-Level One

Four Learning Units to be done by the student at home		Four Examination Units to be administered by the teacher at the lesson	
Each Unit contains:		**Each Unit contains:**	
4 Learning Modules Each module covers the following skill areas:		**2 Tests** **Midterm:** to be completed after Module 2 **Final:** to be completed after Module 4	
Brainthumpers	Quick drills on leaps, articulation, dynamics, fingering, and intervals	**Technic**	Pentascales, triads, and variants
Technic	Pentascale and triad patterns and variants to be practiced daily in set keys with a metronome	**Sightreading**	Short examples, with skills checklist
Prepared Sightreading	Questions and a short musical excerpt	**Aural Skills-Rhythmic**	Beat Clap-Along Echo Clap
Aural Skills-Rhythmic	Clapping (metrical), and rhythmic patterns	**Aural Skills-Pitch**	Interval Sing Echo-Sing
Aural Skills-Pitch	Triad, interval, and echo singing		

Some Basic Tips

Singing Vocalizing has not always been part of traditional piano lessons. Yet recent research has clearly established its importance for developing crucial listening and audiating skills.

Teaching and learning singing in this context is not hard, but does take patience. Many students have not sung and will need some time and work in order to get comfortable. Stick with it! Studies have shown that even those who seem totally tone-deaf on the first attempt can improve significantly with practice.

- Check that posture is good, breathing deep and even, and throat relaxed.
- If the student is having trouble matching pitch, ask them to sing a note and hold it. Find the same pitch and sing it with them. Then ask them to move their voice with you as you sing to the correct pitch.
- Visual and verbal feedback is crucial. Saying "higher" or "lower", or moving your hand up or down to help them find the pitch is a great help.

Technic Technic should be practiced daily. Vary the focus of each week's assignment using the Technic Box in each Module.

- **Fill in the blanks** for the metronome marking (M.M.), the number of the exercise, and hands separate (S) or together (T).
- **Circle** the chosen key(s), articulation(s), and dynamic(s).

Technical exercises are set out in C Major in the last few pages of this book. For students who work better from a printed page, consider using the *Level 1 Technic Book* for the other keys.

Sightreading The word "sightreading" is a misnomer; a better term might be "pattern recognition" or even "flash learning". A good sightreader recognizes familiar patterns in new arrangments; he or she is able to think ahead, keep going despite mistakes, and keep a steady beat.

Here are some steps that have helped my students improve their sightreading:

- Play the piece at a slow tempo without stopping. After finishing, go back and circle mistakes. This builds both analysis and musical memory skills.
- Play slowly again and try to fix all the mistakes – and not add any new ones!
- Play a third time, counting out loud. This time it should be error free.

Steps may be repeated as necessary.

Mix Do you have to do all the activities for every section? You'll make the right decision based on available time, skill level and long-term goals. Remember, the most important factor in improving fundamentals is: **work on them — and do it often!!**